DR. FANATOMY

FAST & SIMPLE
COOKBOOK
FOR TEENS ON-THE-GO

77 EASY & STEP-BY-STEP RECIPE HOW-TO
COOKBOOK FOR TEEN CHEFS

Colored Interior 80 + Photos

© Copyright 2023 - All rights reserved.

The content contained within this book may not be reproduced, duplicated or transmitted without direct written permission from the author or the publisher.

Under no circumstances will any blame or legal responsibility be held against the publisher, or author, for any damages, reparation, or monetary loss due to the information contained within this book, either directly or indirectly.

Legal Notice:
This book is copyright protected. It is only for personal use. You cannot amend, distribute, sell, use, quote, or paraphrase any part, or the content within this book, without the author or publisher's consent.

Disclaimer Notice:
Please note the information contained within this document is for educational and entertainment purposes only. All effort has been executed to present accurate, up-to-date, reliable, complete information. No warranties of any kind are declared or implied. Readers acknowledge that the author is not engaged in the rendering of legal, financial, medical or professional advice. The content within this book has been derived from various sources. Please consult a licensed professional before attempting any techniques outlined in this book.

By reading this document, the reader agrees that under no circumstances is the author responsible for any losses, direct or indirect, that are incurred as a result of the use of the information contained within this document, including, but not limited to, errors, omissions, or inaccuracies.

Bonus Booklet For You!

With great pleasure, I extend a warm welcome to you on your purchase of the book in this TeeNavigator series. Congratulations on stepping towards improving yourself and developing the skills necessary to thrive as a teenager and beyond.

Below is a surprise gift for you!

Download it from the link (or scan the QR code below) - https://bit.ly/TeeNavigationBonus

TABLE OF CONTENTS

INTRODUCTION

1: RISE AND SHINE : (5-27)
Quick and Delicious Breakfast Recipes for Busy Teens

2: QUICK BITES AND TASTY SIDES : (28-56)
Delicious Snacks and Appetizers

3: THE HEALTHY ZONE : (57- 71)
Delicious Soup and Salads for Teens

4: MEAL ON THE RUN: (72-103)
Fast and Easy Meals for Busy Teenagers

5: SWEET TREATS FOR BUSY TEENS : (104-122)
Dessert on the Go

Conclusion

INTRODUCTION

Do you ever look at your parents in the kitchen and wonder how they do it?

Perhaps it's videos on YouTube, cooking shows on television, or even reels on Instagram. Do you see people cook and wonder how they do it?

There may have been instances when you wanted to cook like chefs on TV. Or you may want to become more self-sufficient and independent.

Maybe you want to learn to cook. Whatever your reason, this is the perfect book for you!

Cooking might seem intimidating. After all, there are a variety of techniques, different ingredients, and equipment, and let's remember some basic skills. The good news is that there is always time to learn. You can pick up any skill you want if you desire to learn.

This stands true for cooking as well. As with anything else in life, you need to first start with the basics before moving on to cooking full-fledged meals. It becomes incredibly simple if you have an internal desire to learn.

Learning to cook is a wonderful life skill, even if it is only a couple of basic dishes. Cooking is not only easy but quite an exciting process too. All the time spent in the kitchen will be worth the delicious food you whip up. Also, don't worry if it sounds a little intimidating. You will feel differently once you start cooking through the different recipes in this book. Also, whenever you are learning something new, focus on the benefits you stand to gain. Doing this automatically makes the process and effort involved seem worth it. So, why should you learn to cook?

The first reason is that cooking is an essential life skill. Sure, you can depend on ready-to-cook meals and takeout. However, it is unhealthy and a costly option in the long run. Once you start cooking, your monthly expenditure will be down to the ingredients needed. Even if you save $50 per month by cooking at home, it adds up to $600 by the end of the year! Now, imagine all the money you can save over the years! So cooking at home is budget-friendly!

Another reason to cook at home is it gives you a better insight into where your food comes from. This, in turn, is needed for developing a positive and healthy relationship with food. Also, when you cook at home, you have complete control over the ingredients' quality and their quantities. This is the simplest means to ensure you are consuming healthy meals. Attention to your food choices is needed to improve your overall well-being and health.

Once you start cooking, you will automatically have better control over your nutrition. Do you know that cooking can be a stressbuster or even a hobby? Another benefit of cooking regularly at home is it improves your self-confidence.

When you try something new, it broadens your horizons. You might end up with a new hobby! Learning to shop for, cook, prep, and serve a meal will give you a sense of accomplishment. You can take pride in the efforts made in the kitchen. This simple act helps improve your belief in yourself. It will increase your self-confidence even if it doesn't seem like a big deal. This renewed self-confidence will positively affect all aspects of your life. You can also become a productive and contributing member of your household. So, there is a lot you can gain by learning to cook! If you are starting with cooking, this book will act as your guide every step of the way. It is filled with simple and easy-to-cook recipes. As long as you stick to the instructions given in the recipes, you can whip up delicious meals within no time! All you need to do is go through the different recipes in this book and note the ones that strike your fancy.

After this, check whether your pantry is stocked with the required ingredients. Once both these steps are taken care of, you simply need to follow the instructions in the particular recipe.

If you are eager to start cooking, prepare delicious meals for your loved ones, or improve your cooking skills, there is no time to get started! However, before you try your hand at the different recipes in this book, spend some time to master the basics of cooking too. From meal prepping, planning, and grocery shopping to some simple and essential cooking techniques, all the information needed is given in this book. When in doubt, refer to the basics and get going. Keep an open mind to cooking, and don't hesitate to experiment in the kitchen. Also, remember to have fun!

So, what are you waiting for?

Let's get started immediately!

Dr. Fanatomy

1. RISE AND SHINE

Quick and Delicious Breakfast Recipes for Busy Teens

(1) Quickie Mango Smoothie

Serves: 1

Ingredients:
- ¼ cup unsweetened pineapple juice
- ¼ medium banana, sliced
- ½ tablespoon honey
- 1 cup frozen chopped peeled, mangoes
- ¼ cup plain yogurt

Directions:
- Place pineapple juice, banana, honey, mangoes, and yogurt in a blender.
- Blend until smooth.
- Pour into a glass and serve.

(2) Berry Smoothie

Serves: 1

Ingredients:
- ½ ripe banana
- 1/3 cup of milk of your choice
- ¼ cup plain yogurt
- ¼ cup ripe berries of your choice
- ½ tablespoon honey or maple syrup or agave nectar

Directions:
- Place berries, yogurt, milk, banana, and sweetener in a blender.
- Blend until smooth.
- Pour into a glass and serve.

(3) Copycat Orange Julius Orange Smoothie

Serves: 3

Ingredients:
- 8 ounces of frozen orange juice concentrate
- ¼ cup sugar
- Ice cubes, as required
- ½ cup milk
- ½ teaspoon vanilla
- ½ cup water

Directions:
- Place orange juice concentrate, sugar, ice, milk, vanilla, and water in a high-speed blender.
- Blend until smooth.
- Pour into two glasses and serve.

(4) Copycat McDonald's Strawberry Banana Smoothie

Serves: 1

Ingredients:
- ½ cup crushed ice
- 5 ounces frozen sliced strawberries
- ¼ cup banana slices

Directions:
- Place strawberries, ice, and banana slices in a blender.
- Blend until smooth.
- Pour into a glass and serve.

(5) Donuts Salted Caramel Hot Chocolate

Serves: 4

Ingredients:
- 1 1/3 cups cocoa powder
- 1 1/3 cups water
- 4 – 8 tablespoons salted caramel syrup
- ½ cup whipped cream
- 1 1/3 cups sugar
- 4 cups milk
- Eight tablespoons of caramel syrup
- Salt to garnish

Directions:
- Add water, sugar, and cocoa powder into a saucepan and whisk well.
- Place the saucepan over medium heat. Stir often until the sugar dissolves completely.
- When it starts boiling, turn down the heat and simmer for a couple of minutes. Whisk often.
- Pour milk and stir. Heat thoroughly.
- Pour two tablespoons of salted caramel into each glass or mug.
- Pour hot chocolate into the glasses. Spoon some whipped cream on top.
- Drizzle caramel sauce on top. Sprinkle salt on top and serve.

(6) Yogurt Parfait

Serves: 4

Ingredients:

- 2 cups plain, unsweetened yogurt
- ½ cup chopped mixed fruits of your choice
- ½ cup mixed berries of your choice (chop the larger berries if using)
- Two teaspoons honey
- 1 cup muesli
- Two teaspoons chia seeds
- 1 cup dry roasted nuts (mixture of almonds, pistachios, and walnuts)

Directions :

- Add muesli, honey, yogurt, and chia seeds into a bowl and stir well. Cover and let it be for the next 10 minutes. Then, stir in the fruits and berries.

- Divide the mixture into four bowls. Decorate with nuts and serve.

(7) Fruity Waffle with Peanut Butter

Serves: 4

Ingredients:

- 4 whole-grain waffles

- 2 cups chopped mixed fruits
- 1 cup peanut butter
- 4 tablespoons seeds and nuts trail mix

Directions :

- Spread peanut butter on the waffles. Scatter fruits over the waffles, followed by trail mix.
- Serve right away with a smoothie or milk, or hot chocolate.

8) Egg Salad Sandwich

Serves: 2

Ingredients:

- 4 rye bread slices or any other bread slices of your choice

- 4 tablespoons Greek yogurt or mayonnaise
- 2 stalks of celery, chopped
- 2 cups sliced lettuce leaves
- Salt to taste
- Pepper to taste
- 4 eggs
- 2 tablespoons mustard sauce
- ½ cup minced onions
- 1 teaspoon fresh lemon juice

Directions:

- To boil eggs: Place eggs in a pot. Cover with water. Place the pot over high heat. Cover the pot.
- Let the water come to a rolling boil. Turn off the heat, and do not uncover for about 15 minutes.
- Drain off the water and pour cold water into the pot. Let the eggs sit for a couple of minutes. Peel the eggs and use them as required.
- Place the eggs in a bowl. Crumble the eggs with a fork. Stir in mustard sauce, yogurt, pepper, salt, onion, celery, and lemon juice.
- Toast the bread slices to the desired crispiness in the toaster.
- Place 2 bread slices on a serving platter. Spread lettuce on them. Divide the egg salad mixture equally and place it over the lettuce.
- Cover with the remaining bread slices. Serve right away. You can serve it with a milkshake or smoothie, or hot chocolate.

9) Deviled Egg with Toast

Serves: 4

Ingredients:

- 4 whole-grain bread slices
- 1 cup Greek yogurt
- 2 teaspoons mustard sauce
- 1 cup chopped fresh parsley
- Salt to taste
- Pepper to taste
- 4 hard-boiled eggs
- 2 teaspoons lemon juice
- 1 teaspoon garlic powder
- 2 teaspoons mixed dried herbs

To serve:
- Yogurt
- Chopped fruit of your choice
- Chopped nuts of your choice

Directions:
- Refer to the previous recipe on how to boil eggs. Peel and cut the eggs into 2 halves lengthwise.
- Carefully remove the yolks and add them to a bowl. Keep the whites on a plate.
- Add lemon juice, seasonings, Greek yogurt, and mustard sauce to the bowl of yolks and mix with a fork.
- Fill this mixture into the cavities of the whites.
- Toast the bread slices to the desired crispiness. Place the devilled eggs on top of the toast and serve with yogurt, fruits, and nuts (mix them in a bowl).

10) Quick Oatmeal

Serves: 1

Ingredients:

- ½ cup rolled oats
- ½ cup mashed banana
- 1 tablespoon chopped nuts of your choice
- ¼ teaspoon ground cinnamon
- 1 ½ cups unsweetened almond milk
- ½ tablespoon seeds and nuts trail mix
- ¼ teaspoon vanilla bean paste or vanilla extract

Directions:

- Add oats, bananas, nuts, cinnamon, almond milk, seeds, nuts trail mix, and vanilla into a saucepan.
- Place the saucepan over medium heat. When the mixture starts boiling, reduce the heat and simmer until your preferred consistency is thick. Stir constantly.
- Pour into a bowl. It can be served hot or cold or warm with fresh fruit.

11) Bagel with Cream Cheese

Serves: 2

Ingredients:

- 2 bagels, split, toasted

Topping #1:
- 4 tablespoons blueberry cream cheese spread
- 4 tablespoons coconut flakes
- ½ cup blueberries

Topping # 2:
- 4 tablespoons herbs and spices cream cheese spread
- 4 turkey pepperoni slices
- 2 teaspoons Italian seasoning
- 6 grape or cherry tomatoes, halved
- 4 tablespoons chopped onion

Topping # 3:
- 4 tablespoons Mediterranean garden cream cheese spread
- 4 kalamata olives, pitted, finely chopped
- 2 roasted red peppers packed in water, finely chopped
- ¼ cup finely chopped fresh basil

Topping # 4:
- 3 tablespoons of original cream cheese spread
- 3 tablespoons peanut butter
- Grated or shaved chocolate to garnish
- 1 banana, sliced

Directions:

- Choose any toppings (#1 to 4). Then, spread cream cheese on the cut part of the bagels.
- Place the toppings over the cream cheese layer and serve.

12) French Toast

Serves: 6

Ingredients:

- 12 slices thick bread
- 1 cup milk
- 6 tablespoons all-purpose flour
- ⅛ teaspoon salt

- 4 eggs
- 4 teaspoons vanilla extract
- 2 tablespoons granulated sugar
- 6 teaspoons butter

To serve: Optional
- Butter
- Honey
- Powdered sugar
- Syrup
- Fruits and berries of your choice

Directions:

- Add eggs into a bowl and whisk until frothy. Add vanilla, salt, milk, and flour to whisk well.
- Place a large nonstick pan over medium heat. Add butter and allow it to melt. Swirl the pan to spread the butter.
- Dip the bread slices in the egg mixture, one at a time, and place it in the pan. Place as many as can fit in the pan.
- Cook until the underside is golden brown. Flip sides and cook the other side until golden brown. Transfer onto a plate. Cook the remaining bread slices in a similar manner.
- Serve with any of the suggested serving options.

13) Breakfast Pizza

Serves: 2 – 4

Ingredients:

- 2 – 4 whole-wheat English muffins, split
- 1 cup finely chopped onion
- ½ cup thinly sliced bell peppers of any color
- 4 tablespoons pizza sauce
- 8 tablespoons olive oil
- 1 cup thinly sliced tomato
- ½ cup boiled corn kernels
- 2 cups shredded mozzarella cheese
- 2 tablespoons mixed dried herbs

Directions:

- Preheat the oven to 400° F. Prepare a baking sheet by lining it with parchment paper.
- Lay the muffin halves on the prepared baking sheet. Drizzle olive oil on the cut part of each English muffin. Bake for 4 – 5 minutes or until light brown.
- Spread pizza sauce on each muffin half. Next, sprinkle onion, bell pepper, tomato, and corn over the pizza halves.
- Spread pizza sauce on each muffin half. Next, sprinkle onion, bell pepper, tomato, and corn over the pizza halves.

Directions:

- Preheat the oven to 400° F. Prepare a baking sheet by lining it with parchment paper.
- Lay the muffin halves on the prepared baking sheet. Drizzle olive oil on the cut part of each English muffin. Bake for 4 – 5 minutes or until light brown.
- Spread pizza sauce on each muffin half. Next, sprinkle onion, bell pepper, tomato, and corn over the pizza halves.
- Spread pizza sauce on each muffin half. Next, sprinkle onion, bell pepper, tomato, and corn over the pizza halves.
- Next, sprinkle the mixed herbs, followed by cheese. Place the baking sheet in the oven and bake for 10 minutes or until the cheese melts and is brown at a few spots.
- Serve.

14) Ham and Cheddar Cheese Muffins

Serves: 6

Ingredients:

- 5 large eggs
- Pepper to taste
- Salt to taste
- ¼ teaspoon garlic powder
- ¼ teaspoon dried mustard or Dijon mustard
- ¼ teaspoon onion powder
- 1/3 cup grated cheddar cheese plus extra to top
- 1/3 cup chopped cooked or deli ham

Directions:

- Set the oven temperature to 350 °F and preheat the oven.
- Grease a 6-count muffin pan with some cooking spray. You can also line them with disposable liners.
- Beat eggs in a bowl, adding salt and pepper to taste.
- Add cheese, ham, garlic powder, mustard, and onion powder and whisk well.
- Distribute the egg mixture into the muffin cups.
- Sprinkle some cheddar cheese on top if desired, and place the muffin pan in the oven.
- Set the timer for 12 to 15 minutes or until the muffins are firm.
- Let the muffins cool for 3 – 4 minutes before serving.

(15) Cheesy Eggs in the Hole With Bacon

Serves: 2

Ingredients:

- 2 slices bacon
- 2 thick bread slices (½ inch thick slices)
- 2 tablespoons grated parmesan cheese
- ½ tablespoon unsalted butter
- 2 large eggs
- Salt to taste
- Pepper to taste

Directions:

- Take a cookie cutter about 2 ½ inches in diameter and cut out bread from the center of each slice. You want a hole in the center of each bread slice, big enough to fit an egg.
- Place a nonstick pan over medium-high heat. Add bacon and cook until crisp.
- Remove the bacon with a slotted spoon and place it on a plate lined with paper towels.
- Do not drain the fat from the pan; stir in the butter.
- Now brush this butter-bacon fat mixture over the bread slices (the cut and the hole parts) and place them on the skillet. Cook until light brown. Turn the bread slices with a hole and cut the piece over)
- Break an egg into each hole and top with Parmesan cheese.
- After cooking for about 2 minutes, turn the slices with egg and cut part over. Cook until the eggs are cooked to your preference, but runny yolks taste great. The cut part of the bread can be dipped in the runny yolks. Sprinkle salt and pepper to taste.
- Transfer onto a plate. Crumble the bacon over the eggs.
- Serve.

(16)Pancakes

Serves: 6

Ingredients:

Pancakes:
- 1 large egg
- 1 ⅛ cups self-rising flour
- 1 cup milk

Add-ins (optional):
- 1 teaspoon sugar or more to taste
- ½ teaspoon vanilla extract
- 1 teaspoon baking powder
- 2 – 3 tablespoons chocolate chips
- ⅛ teaspoon salt
- ¼ cup blueberries or raspberries

Directions:

- Crack the egg into a bowl. Add milk and beat until well incorporated.
- If you want to add any optional add-ins, add them now and stir until well combined.
- Place a nonstick pan over medium-low heat. When the pan is hot, spray the pan with some cooking spray.
- Scoop out about 1/3 cup of batter and place it on the pan. Soon bubbles will be visible on top of the pancake.
- Slightly lift a part of the edge and check the color of the pancake. Flip the pancake over and cook the other side when golden brown.
- Remove the pancake onto a plate and serve with toppings of your choice, like butter, syrup, ice cream, etc.
- Make the remaining pancakes similarly.

2. QUICK BITES AND TASTY SIDES

Delicious Snacks and Appetizers

Snacks

(17) Apple Sandwiches

Serves: 2 – 3

Ingredients:
- 1 apple, cored, cut into thin slices
- Peanut butter or almond butter, as required

Directions:
- Spread peanut butter on half the apple slices.
- Cover with the remaining apple slices and serve.

(18) Dark Chocolate Cherry Trail Mix

Serves: 6

Ingredients:
- ¾ cup roasted salted almonds
- ½ cup dried cherries
- ¾ cup raw cashews
- ½ - 1/3 cup dark chocolate chips

Directions:
- Combine nuts, cherries, and chocolate chips in an airtight container.
- Place it at room temperature.

(19) Energy Bites

Serves: 8

Ingredients:

- ½ cup pitted dried dates
- ⅛ cup old-fashioned rolled oats
- 1 tablespoon almond flour or almond meal
- ½ tablespoon maple syrup
- 2 tablespoons unsweetened cocoa powder
- ⅛ cup unsalted cashews or any other nuts of your choice
- A pinch of sea salt (optional)

Directions:

- Place all the dry ingredients in the food processor bowl and process until coarsely chopped.
- Drizzle maple syrup through the feeder tube with the food processor machine running.
- Process until just combined, and the mixture sticks together when you press some of it in your fist.
- Divide the mixture into 8 equal portions and shape it into balls.
- You can serve it right away or transfer into an airtight container and store it at room temperature. It can last for 5 – 6 days.

(20) Chocolate Cherry Protein Smoothie

Serves: 1

Ingredients:

- ½ cup pitted sweet cherries
- ½ banana, sliced
- 1 tablespoon cocoa powder
- ½ teaspoon vanilla extract
- ½ cup cottage cheese
- 3 tablespoons chocolate protein powder
- 1 tablespoon flaxseed meal

Directions:

- Blend all the ingredients in a blender until smooth.
- Serve with ice.

(21) Nut Butter and Banana Open-Face Sandwich

Serves: 2

Ingredients:
- 2 slices of bread of your choice, preferably multigrain or Ezekiel
- 2 tablespoons honey
- 2 small bananas, sliced
- Nut butter of your choice, like peanut or almond, etc.

Directions:
- Spread nut butter on the bread slices.
- Place banana slices on top. Drizzle honey over the banana layer and serve.

(22) Italian Cream Cheese Stuffed Celery

Serves: 4

Ingredients:
- 3 – 4 stalks of celery, rinsed, cut into 3-inch pieces
- ½ package (from a 0.7-ounce package) of Italian dressing mix
- ½ cup shredded mozzarella cheese
- 4 ounces of cream cheese, softened
- ¼ cup mayonnaise
- Paprika to garnish

Directions:

- Add cream cheese, mayonnaise, Italian dressing mix, and cheese into a bowl and mix well.
- Fill this mixture with the celery sticks. Garnish with paprika and serve.

(23) Cheese and Crackers

Serves: 4

Ingredients:
- 4 cheese slices
- 4 crackers

Toppings: Optional
- Fresh or dried fruit of your choice, chopped
- Chopped nuts
- Chopped fresh herbs of your choice
- Jam or jelly or honey

Directions:

- Add cream cheese, mayonnaise, Italian dressing mix, and cheese into a bowl and mix well.
- Fill this mixture with the celery sticks. Garnish with paprika and serve.

(24) Baked Tomatoes with Mozzarella and Parmesan

Serves: 2-3

Ingredients:
- 4 cheese slices
- 4 crackers

Toppings: Optional
- 2 Roma tomatoes, cut into round slices
- ½ cup shredded parmesan cheese
- Olive oil to drizzle
- ½ cup shredded mozzarella cheese
- ¼ cup chopped fresh basil

Directions:

- Preheat the oven to 350° F.
- Line a baking sheet with parchment paper and place the tomato slices over it.
- Sprinkle Parmesan over the tomatoes, followed by mozzarella cheese. Garnish with basil.
- Trickle oil on top and place it in the oven for 8 to 10 minutes.
- Now set the oven to broil and broil until the cheese is brown at a few spots.

(25) Pigs in a Blanket

Serves: 4

Ingredients:
- 4 hot dogs
- ½ can (8 ounces can) Pillsbury crescent dinner rolls, separate into triangles
- 2 slices American cheese, halved

Directions:

- Preheat the oven to 375° F.
- Place the hot dogs in a microwave-safe bowl and cook on high for 1 minute.
- Make a slit in the center of each hot dog, ensuring it is not cut throughout the hot dog, leaving ½ inch on both ends intact.
- Push a strip of cheese into the slit of each of the hot dogs. Next, take a triangle of the dough and wrap it over the hot dog, leaving the ends of the hot dog. The hot dog should be peeping on either side. Repeat with all the hot dogs.
- Place the pigs in a blanket on a baking sheet and bake for around 15 minutes or until they turn a nice golden brown.
- Cool for about 5 minutes and serve.

(26) Chocolate Peanut Butter Grahams

Serves: 18

Ingredients:

- 9 whole graham crackers, halved
- 6 ounces white chocolate chips
- 6 ounces of milk chocolate chips
- 2 tablespoons creamy peanut butter

Directions:

- Melt white chocolate chips and peanut butter in a microwave-safe bowl in the microwave for about 30 seconds. Stir well and cook for another 10 – 20 seconds or until smooth.
- Prepare a baking sheet by lining it with parchment paper.
- Working with one graham cracker half at a time, dunk half the cracker in the melted mixture and place it on the baking sheet.
- After about 7 – 8 minutes (or when the chocolate mixture sets on the cracker), melt milk chocolate chips in a microwave-safe bowl for about 40 – 50 seconds or until smooth. Stir the chocolate after melting for about 30 seconds.
- Now dunk the other end of the cracker in the milk chocolate and place it on the baking sheet.
- If you have any excess chocolate, put them in a small plastic bag. Cut off a corner of each bag.
- Drizzle the milk chocolate on the white chocolate part of the cracker and vice versa.
- When it sets completely, transfer the crackers into an airtight container.

(27) Peanut Butter Cups

Serves: 6

Ingredients:

- ½ package (from an 11.5 ounces package) of milk chocolate chips divided
- ⅛ teaspoon salt
- ½ cup peanut butter
- ¼ cup powdered sugar sifted

Directions:
- Line 6 cups of a mini muffin pan with disposable liners.
- Melt half the chocolate chips in the microwave in a microwave-safe bowl on high for about a minute or until smooth, stirring halfway through melting.

- Spoon the melted chocolate into the mini muffin cups. With the same spoon, brush the melted chocolate on the sides of the cups. Chill until the chocolate sets.
- Add sugar, peanut butter, and salt into a bowl and stir. Divide this mixture equally and place it over the hardened chocolate.
- Repeat step 2 once again. Spoon the melted chocolate into the mini muffin cups over the peanut butter mixture. Make sure the chocolate covers the peanut butter mixture. You can use a spoon to spread it. Chill until the chocolate hardens.
- Transfer into an airtight container and refrigerate until use.

(28) Famous Hot Chocolate

Serves: 1 – 2

Ingredients:

- 1 cup 2% milk
- ¼ cup cocoa powder
- ½ tablespoon grated milk chocolate
- 5 – 6 drops of vanilla extract
- ¼ cup heavy whipping cream
- ½ tablespoon granulated sugar
- ½ can (from 14 ounces can) of sweetened condensed milk

To top:

- Ground cinnamon
- Whipped topping placed in a piping bag
- Chocolate shaving

Directions:

- Place cream and milk in a saucepan over medium-high heat.
- Add sugar, cocoa, and milk chocolate into another bowl and whisk well.
- Pour the chocolate mixture into the saucepan, whisking constantly.
- Lower the heat to medium heat.
- Stir in vanilla and condensed milk. Lower the heat to low heat and cook for 2 – 3 minutes. Turn off the heat.

- .Pour into mugs.
- Place some whipped topping on top. Garnish with cinnamon and chocolate shavings and serve.

(29) Bisquick Chocolate Chip Muffins

Serves: 24

Ingredients:

- 2 eggs
- 2 ½ cups mashed overripe bananas
- 6 tablespoons vegetable oil

- ⅔ cup sugar
- ⅔ cup miniature semi-sweet chocolate chips
- 4 cups Original Bisquick mix

Directions:

- Preheat the oven to 400° F.
- Prepare 2 muffin pans of 12 counts each with some cooking oil spray. Place disposable liners in each cup.
- Crack eggs into a bowl and whisk lightly.
- Add bananas, oil, sugar, and Bisquick mix and stir until smooth.
- Add chocolate chips and fold gently. Spoon the batter into the muffin cups.
- Place the muffin pans in the oven and set the timer for 15 minutes or until golden brown.
- Cool for about 8 – 10 minutes before taking them off the pans.
- Store in an airtight container. You can refrigerate them, and they can last for 7 – 8 days.

(30) Mexican Bean Dip

Serves: 2 – 3

Ingredients:

- ½ can (from 15 ounces can) of baked beans
- ¼ cup grated cheese
- ½ tablespoon chili sauce or to taste
- ½ can (from 15 ounces can) of kidney beans, drained
- ½ tablespoon Worcestershire sauce

Directions:

- Heat kidney beans in a saucepan for about a minute, mashing as you stir.
- Stir in the baked beans and mash these as well. The dip is to be rough in texture.
- Stir in Worcestershire sauce, cheese, and chili sauce. Turn off the heat and serve it with tortilla chips or corn chips.

(31) Oreo Milkshake

Serves: 4

Ingredients:

- For milkshake:
- 4 cups vanilla ice cream
- 1 1/3 cups milk
- 12 candy corn Oreos, broken

For garnishing: Optional
- Sprinkles
- Whipped cream

Directions:

- Add ice cream, milk, and candy corn Oreos into a blender to make a milkshake.
- Blend until smooth and frothy.
- Pour into glasses and serve.
- Garnish with whipped cream and sprinkles, and serve.

Sides

(32) Creamy Coleslaw

Serves: 3

Ingredients:

- 7 ounces coleslaw mix
- 3 tablespoons sour cream or Greek yogurt
- ½ teaspoon seasoned salt or to taste
- ⅛ teaspoon celery salt
- 6 tablespoons mayonnaise
- 2 tablespoons sugar
- ¼ teaspoon ground mustard

Directions:

- Combine all the ingredients in a bowl and stir. Chill until use.

(33) Copycat Olive Garden Savory Biscuit Breadsticks

Serves: 5

Ingredients:

- ¼ cup grated parmesan cheese
- ⅛ teaspoon crushed red pepper flakes
- 1 tablespoon olive oil
- 1 teaspoon dried minced garlic
- ½ tube (from a 6 ounces tube) of refrigerated buttermilk biscuits

Directions:

- Preheat the oven to 400° F. Grease a baking sheet with cooking spray.
- Add cheese, pepper flakes, and garlic into a bowl and stir.
- Take out the biscuits one at a time and roll them into a log of about 6 inches. Brush oil over the biscuit. Dredge in cheese mixture and place on the baking sheet.
- Place the baking sheet in the oven and set the timer for 8 to 10 minutes or until they turn golden brown.
- Cool for a few minutes and serve.

(34) Creamy Corn

Serves: 4

Ingredients:

- 3 cups frozen corn, thawed
- 3 tablespoons butter, cut into cubes
- ¼ teaspoon salt
- 4 ounces cream cheese, cut into cubes
- ¼ teaspoon garlic powder
- ⅛ teaspoon pepper

Directions:

- Add corn, butter, seasonings, and cream cheese to a heavy pan. Place the pan over low heat and cover it with a lid. Heat thoroughly. Stir on and off until the cream cheese melts.
- Mix well and serve.

(35) Parmesan Potato Wedges

Serves: 4

Ingredients:

- ⅛ cup grated parmesan cheese
- ¼ teaspoon garlic powder
- ¼ teaspoon paprika
- ½ teaspoon garlic salt
- ¼ teaspoon dried oregano
- 1 pound medium baking potatoes, peel if desired, cut each into 8 wedges lengthwise

Directions:

- Preheat the oven to 400° F.
- Combine cheese and seasonings in a bowl.
- Line a baking dish with parchment paper. Place the potato wedges in the baking dish. Spray with cooking spray. Sprinkle the spice mixture over the potatoes.
- Keep the baking dish in the oven and set the timer for 30 minutes or until tender and can be pierced easily with a fork.

(36) Stir-fried Broccoli

Serves: 2-3

Ingredients:

- 1 large head of broccoli, cut into florets
- 1 tablespoon olive oil
- ⅛ cup crumbled feta cheese (optional)
- 1 onion, thinly sliced
- ¼ teaspoon salt
- Freshly ground black pepper to taste
- ½ teaspoon dried oregano

Directions:

- Pour oil into a pan and place it over high heat. When the oil is hot, add onion and stir. Cook for about a minute.
- Stir in broccoli and cook for a few minutes until broccoli turns bright green and slightly crisp and tender.
- Add salt, pepper, feta cheese, and oregano and mix well.
- Serve hot.

(37) Mushrooms in Sour Cream Sauce

Serves: 2

Ingredients:

- 1 tablespoon butter
- ½ large onion, finely chopped
- Salt to taste
- Pepper to taste
- ⅛ cup finely chopped fresh dill or parsley (optional)
- ½ pound mushrooms, sliced
- 4 ounces sour cream
- 2 cloves garlic, minced
- Red chili flakes (optional)

Directions:
- Add butter into a skillet and place the skillet over medium-high heat. When butter melts, add onion and garlic and stir. Cook until the onion turns translucent.
- Stir in the mushrooms and cook for a few minutes until it releases moisture and is slightly tender.
- Stir in the sour cream, salt, and pepper and let it simmer on low heat for about 5 minutes or until the thickness you prefer. Sprinkle red chili flakes if using, and serve.

(38) Garlic Mashed Red Potatoes

Serves: 3

Ingredients:

- 4 medium red potatoes, peeled, quartered
- 1 tablespoon butter
- ¼ teaspoon salt
- 2 cloves garlic, peeled
- ¼ cup warm fat-free milk
- ⅛ cup grated parmesan cheese

Directions:

- Add garlic and potatoes to a pot. Pour enough water to cover the potatoes.
- Place the pot over high heat. When water starts boiling, turn down the heat and cook covered until very soft.
- Drain off the water from the pot. Mash the potatoes along with milk, butter, salt, and cheese. Transfer into a bowl and serve.

(39) Honey Garlic Green Beans

Serves: 4

Ingredients:

- 2 tablespoons honey
- 2 cloves garlic, minced
- 1/8 teaspoon crushed red pepper flakes
- 1 tablespoon of low-sodium soy sauce
- 1/8 teaspoon salt
- 1 pound fresh green beans, trimmed

Directions:

- Boil a pot of water. When the water starts boiling, add the beans and cook for 2 to 3 minutes or until they are crisp and tender.
- Drain the beans in a colander and immerse their beans in a bowl of ice water for about 5 minutes. Drain well.
- Combine honey, garlic, red pepper flakes, soy sauce, and salt in a bowl.
- Place a pan over medium-high heat. Spray the pan with some cooking spray.
- Add beans and cook for a few minutes until you find some blisters on the beans. Stir occasionally.
- Stir in the sauce. Keep stirring until the sauce thickens and coats the beans.
- Transfer into a serving dish and serve.

(40) Peas with Lemon

Serves: 2

Ingredients:

- 1 cup frozen peas, thawed
- ½ tablespoon salted butter
- Salt to taste
- ¼ teaspoon grated lemon rind
- 1 clove garlic, peeled, smashed
- ½ tablespoon olive oil
- Freshly ground pepper to taste

Directions:

- Smash the garlic cloves using a mortar and pestle.

- Drain off any water from the peas.
- Place a skillet over medium-high heat with oil and butter in it.
- When the butter melts, stir in the garlic and cook for a few seconds until it is light brown.
- Stir in the peas and heat thoroughly. Stir in the lemon rind, salt, and pepper.
- Pick up the garlic cloves and discard them. Serve.

(41) Classic Garlic Bread

Serves: 4

Ingredients:

- ½ loaf French bread halved lengthwise
- 2 cloves garlic, peeled, minced, or finely grated

- 1 tablespoon grated parmesan cheese or more if you like it cheesy
- 2 tablespoons melted, salted butter
- ½ tablespoon finely chopped fresh parsley
- Salt to taste

Directions:
- Preheat the oven to 400° F.
- Add butter, garlic, and parsley into a bowl and stir. Brush the butter over the cut part of the bread. Season with salt.
- Take a large sheet of foil, wrap the loaf halves together (their original shape), and place them on a baking sheet.
- Keep the baking sheet in the oven and set the timer for 8 minutes.
- Unwrap and place the bread halves on the baking sheet, with the cut side facing on top.
- Top with Parmesan cheese. Set the oven to broil and place the baking sheet in the oven. Broil until crispy and brown. Slice and serve.

3. THE HEALTHY ZONE

Delicious Soup and Salads for Teens

Soups

(42) Cracker Potato Soup

Serves: 6

Ingredients:

- 1 ½ pounds potatoes, peeled, cubed
- 4 cups water
- ¼ teaspoon pepper
- 2 ½ cups milk
- ½ cup all-purpose flour
- 4 ounces celery, chopped
- 2 ounces of chicken base
- ½ tablespoon salt
- 2 ounces margarine, melted

Directions:

- Combine water, celery, potatoes, seasonings, and chicken base in a soup pot. Place the pot over high heat.
- When the mixture starts boiling, boil the heat to low and simmer until the potatoes are cooked and soft.
- Stir in the milk. Whisk together flour and margarine in a bowl.
- Now check the temperature of the milk. When the soup temperature is 170° F, pour 2 cups into the bowl with the flour mixture and whisk well. Pour it back into the pot and keep whisking until well combined.
- Cook for about 20 minutes, stirring occasionally.
- Ladle into soup bowls and serve.

(43) Chicken Soup

Serves: 3

Ingredients:

- 1 can (14.5 ounces) of chicken broth
- ½ package (from a 16 ounces package) of frozen mixed vegetables
- 1 can (10.75 ounces) reduced-fat, reduced-sodium condensed cream of chicken soup (do not dilute)
- 1 tablespoon finely chopped onion
- 1 cup cooked, cubed chicken breast

Directions:

- Pour broth into a saucepan. Place the saucepan over high heat. Add the vegetables, pepper, and tortellini when the broth starts boiling. Cook until pasta is al dente.
- Serve in bowls garnished with basil.

(44) Tortellini Primavera Soup

Serves: 2

Ingredients:

- 4 cups chicken broth
- ½ package (from a 9 ounces package) of refrigerated cheese tortellini

- ⅛ teaspoon pepper
- ½ package (from a 10 ounces package) of julienne-cut carrots
- ½ cup frozen peas
- Thinly sliced fresh basil leaves to garnish

Directions:

- Pour broth into a saucepan. Place the saucepan over high heat. Add the vegetables, pepper, and tortellini when the broth starts boiling. Cook until pasta is al dente.

- Serve in bowls garnished with basil.

(45) Tomato Hamburger Soup

Serves: 6

Ingredients:

- ½ can (from 46 ounces can) of V8 juice
- ½ pound ground beef
- 1 teaspoon dried minced onion
- 1 package (16 ounces) of frozen mixed vegetables
- ½ can (from 10.75 ounces can) condensed cream of mushroom soup (do not dilute)
- Salt to taste
- Pepper to taste

Directions:

- Place beef into a pot or Dutch oven over medium heat.
- Cook until brown. As you stir, crumble the meat into smaller pieces.
- Add the rest of the ingredients and stir. When the mixture starts boiling, turn down the heat and simmer for about 30 minutes or until the vegetables are tender. Stir on and off. Add salt and pepper to taste and stir.
- Ladle into soup bowls and serve.

Salads

(46) Watermelon Caprese Salad

Serves: 3

Ingredients:

- 2 ounces fresh mozzarella cheese, cubed
- ⅛ teaspoon pepper
- ⅛ cup thinly sliced fresh basil
- ½ tablespoon extra-virgin olive oil (optional)
- ⅛ teaspoon salt
- 2 cups seedless watermelon cubes
- ½ tablespoon balsamic vinegar

Directions:

- Place mozzarella cheese in a bowl. Sprinkle salt and pepper and toss.
- Stir in basil and watermelon. Pour oil and vinegar and toss well

(47) Apple Pomegranate Salad

Serves: 4

Ingredients:

- 4 cups torn Romaine lettuce
- ¼ cup chopped pecans or walnuts

- ½ large Granny Smith apple, cored, chopped
- 2 tablespoons olive oil
- 1 tablespoon sugar
- ¼ cup pomegranate seeds
- ¼ cup shredded parmesan cheese
- ½ tablespoon lemon juice
- 2 tablespoons white wine vinegar
- ⅛ teaspoon salt

Directions:

- Preheat the oven up to 350° F and spread the nuts on a baking sheet.
- Keep the baking sheet in the oven and bake the nuts for 5 – 8 minutes, until light brown. Keep a watch over the nuts after 5 minutes, as they can burn.
- Cool the nuts completely.
- Combine apple and lemon juice in a bowl. The lemon juice prevents the apple from turning brown.
- To make the dressing: Whisk together oil, sugar, vinegar, and salt in a bowl.
- Add lettuce, pomegranate, and Parmesan cheese to the bowl of apples.
- Pour the dressing over the salad. Toss well and serve.

(48) Strawberry Feta Tossed Salad

Serves: 3

Ingredients:

- 3 cups torn, mixed salad greens
- 2 ounces feta cheese, crumbled
- Balsamic vinaigrette to taste
- 1 cup sliced fresh strawberries
- ⅛ cup sunflower seed kernels

Directions:

- Combine salad greens, feta, strawberries, and sunflower seeds in a bowl.
- Pour around 2 tablespoons of the vinaigrette and toss well. Taste a bit of the salad and add more vinaigrette if required.

(48) Candy Bar Apple Salad

Serves: 6

Ingredients:

- ¾ cup cold milk
- ½ carton (from an 8 ounces carton) of frozen whipped topping, thawed

- 2 snickers candy bars, cut into ½ inch pieces
- ½ package (from a 3.4 ounces package) of instant vanilla pudding mix
- 2 large apples, cored, chopped

Directions:

- Add milk and pudding mixture into a bowl and whisk well. Do not disturb it for 2 to 3 minutes until it is slightly set.
- Add whipped topping and fold gently. Add apples and candy bars and fold gently.
- Cover the bowl with cling wrap and chill until ready to serve.

(49) Colorful Spiral Pasta Salad

Serves: 6

Ingredients:

- 6 ounces tricolor spiral pasta
- 1 cup grape tomatoes
- Salt to taste
- ¾ cup Italian salad dressing with roasted red pepper and parmesan cheese
- 2 cups fresh broccoli florets
- ½ can (from 6 ounces can) of pitted ripe olives, drained
- Pepper to taste

Directions:

- Follow the directions given on the package of pasta and cook the pasta. Add broccoli for 2 minutes before draining the pasta.
- Place pasta with olives, tomatoes, pepper, and salt in a bowl. Toss well. Pour the dressing over the salad. Toss well and refrigerate until ready to serve.

(50) Pear & Blue Cheese Salad

Serves: 5

Ingredients:

- 6 cups torn Romaine lettuce leaves
- 1 pear, peeled, cored, sliced
- 1/3 cup pecans
- 1/3 cup balsamic vinaigrette
- 1/3 cup crumbled blue cheese

Directions:

- Combine lettuce and balsamic vinaigrette in a bowl. Scatter pear slices, pecans, and cheese on top and serve.

4. MEAL ON THE RUN

Fast and Easy Meals for Busy Teenagers

(51) Grilled Chocochip Sandwich

Serves: 2

Ingredients:

- 4 slices bread
- A handful of milk chocolate chips or 2 milk chocolate bars
- 2 – 3 tablespoons of butter
- 6 large marshmallows

Directions:

- Place a skillet over medium-low heat. Spread butter on one side of each piece of bread.
- Place a slice of bread in the skillet, with the butter side facing down.
- Scatter half the chocolate chips or place a bar of chocolate.
- Squeeze 3 the marshmallows slightly and put them over the chocolate chips. Cover with a slice of bread; the butter side should be facing on top this time.
- Press slightly and cook the sandwich until the underside is golden brown and the chocolate and marshmallows are melted.

- Press the sandwich slightly on and off. Flip sides and cook the other side until golden brown.
- Transfer onto a plate. Cut into the desired shape and serve.
- Make the other sandwich similarly (steps 2 – 6).

(52) Grilled Cheese Sandwich

Serves: 2

Ingredients:

- 2 slices white bread
- 1 slice of cheddar cheese
- 1 ½ - 2 tablespoons butter

Directions:

- Place a skillet over medium heat.
- Spread half the butter on one side of a bread slice and place it in the skillet with the butter side facing down. Next, place the cheese slice on the bread.
- Spread the remaining butter over the other side of the bread and place it on the cheese slice, with the butter side facing on top.
- Cook until the underside is browned, as per your preference. Then, turn the sandwich over and cook the other side as well.
- Transfer the sandwich to a plate. Cut into 2 halves and serve.

(53) Burger Cheddar Melt

Serves: 1

Ingredients:

- 1 ½ tablespoons butter
- ¾ cup milk
- Salt to taste
- 1 burger patty
- 1 tablespoon teriyaki sauce
- 1 ½ tablespoons all-purpose flour
- ½ cup shredded cheddar cheese
- Freshly ground black pepper to taste
- ¼ small onion, finely chopped
- 1 rye bun, split

Directions:

- Place a skillet over medium-low heat. Spread butter on one side of each piece of bread.
- Place a slice of bread in the skillet, with the butter side facing down.
- Scatter half the chocolate chips or place a bar of chocolate.

(54) Fried Rice

Serves: 4

Ingredients:

- 1 ½ cups cooked rice, cooled, preferably leftover rice
- ½ cup chopped onion
- 1 – 1 ½ tablespoons soy sauce or to taste
- 1 green onion, thinly sliced (optional)
- 1 tablespoon vegetable oil or sesame oil
- ½ cup frozen peas and carrots, thawed
- 1 egg, lightly beaten

Directions:

- Not everyone may like the taste of sesame oil. So use sesame only if you want it; otherwise, any vegetable oil you choose will do.
- Pour oil into a skillet or wok and place it over medium heat. When the oil is hot, add onions and stir. Cook for about a minute.
- Stir in peas and carrots and cook for a few minutes until slightly soft.
- Push the vegetables onto one of the sides of the pan. Pour the beaten egg into the pan's center and often stir until the eggs are soft-cooked.
- Now mix the eggs with the vegetables. Stir in the rice and soy sauce. Heat thoroughly, often stirring as it heats.
- Sprinkle green onions if using and stir. Turn off the heat and serve.

(55) Garlic Parmesan Spaghetti

Serves: 4

Ingredients:

- 4 ounces spaghetti
- 2 cloves garlic, peeled, finely chopped
- ¼ teaspoon chicken bouillon powder
- ½ tablespoon chopped Italian parsley
- 1 tablespoon olive oil
- ¼ teaspoon salt
- ⅛ cup grated parmesan cheese or more if you like it cheesy

Directions:

- Follow the directions given on the package and cook the spaghetti.
- Place a skillet over medium heat. Add oil and let it heat. Add garlic and cook for about 30 seconds when the oil is hot, stirring constantly.
- Stir in the spaghetti. Next, sprinkle salt and chicken bouillon powder and give it a good stir. Remove from heat. Stir in the Parmesan.
- Sprinkle parsley on top and serve.

(56) Cracker Mac n Cheese

Serves: 3

Ingredients:

- 3 tablespoons butter
- 1 cup dry macaroni pasta shells
- 1 cup of milk
- 3 tablespoons all-purpose flour
- ½ teaspoon salt
- 1 ¼ cups shredded Colby cheese

Directions:
- Follow the directions given on the package and cook the pasta.
- Keep the oven to broil mode and preheat the oven to medium heat.
- Place a cast-iron skillet or oven-proof over medium heat. Add butter. When butter melts, add flour and keep stirring until roux is formed.
- Add salt, and stir.
- Pour milk, whisking constantly. Keep whisking until the sauce is thick.
- Add half the cheese and stir until the cheese melts. Turn off the heat.
- Stir in the pasta. Sprinkle the remaining cheese on top.
- Shift the skillet into the oven. Make sure to wear oven mitts. Broil for 3 to 4 minutes or until the cheese melts and is browned at a few spots.
- Serve hot.

(57) Chili Cheese Burrito

Serves: 3

Ingredients:

- ½ pound ground beef
- ½ can (from 10 ounces can) of refried beans
- Shredded taco cheese like queso fresco, Cotija, etc., as required
- ½ tablespoon taco seasoning or to taste
- 3 ounces tomato paste
- 3 flour tortillas

Directions:

- Place a skillet over medium heat. Add beef and cook until it is not pink anymore. As you stir, break the meat into crumbles. Discard excess fat from the pan.
- Add taco seasoning and mix well.
- Stir in refried beans and tomato paste. When the mixture is well heated, turn off the heat. Add a little cheese and stir.
- To assemble: Place 1/3 of the mixture on one of the edges of each tortilla. Roll it up and place its seam side facing down on a plate.

- Place a skillet over medium heat. Place a burrito on the pan and press slightly. Cook until the underside is crisp. Turn the burrito over and cook the other side until crispy. Transfer onto a plate and serve with a sauce or dip of your choice.
- Cook the remaining burritos similarly.

(58) Quesadilla

Serves: 4

Ingredients:

- 4 whole-wheat or multigrain tortillas
- 1 cup finely chopped onion

- ½ cup thinly sliced bell pepper
- 2 teaspoons olive oil
- 2 cups grated cheddar cheese
- ½ cup boiled corn
- ½ cup chopped mushrooms
- Seasonings of your choice

Directions:

- Combine the onions, corn, mushrooms, and bell peppers in a bowl.
- Divide the mixture equally and place it over one half of each tortilla.
- Sprinkle ½ cup of cheese over the mixture on each tortilla.
- Fold the other half of the tortilla over the filling (the edges of the tortilla should meet). Do this with each tortilla.
- Place a nonstick pan over medium heat. Brush some oil over the pan. Place a quesadilla in the pan and press lightly. Cook until the underside is crisp. Turn the quesadilla over and cook the other side as well.
- Transfer onto a plate. Cut into wedges to serve with the dip.
- Cook the remaining quesadillas similarly.

(59) Chicken Bacon Ranch Wraps

Serves: 4

Ingredients:

- 2 large tortillas
- 4 strips of thick-cut bacon
- ¼ cup diced tomatoes
- 4 ounces deli sliced chicken breast
- 1 cup sliced lettuce leaves
- 2 tablespoons ranch dressing

Directions:

- Place a pan over medium heat. Add bacon strips into the pan and cook until the underside is crisp. Flip sides and cook the other side until crisp or how you prefer it cooked. Take the bacon from the pan and place it on a plate lined with paper towels.

- Place the tortillas on your countertop or 2 plates. Scatter ½ cup of lettuce leaves (on each tortilla) along the diameter of the tortillas.

- Sprinkle half the tomatoes over the lettuce leaves, followed by a tablespoon of ranch dressing. Divide the chicken as well. Warp the tortilla along with the filling. Cut into two halves if desired and serve.

(60) Chicken Nuggets

Serves: 3

Ingredients:
- 1 ½ skinless, boneless chicken breasts
- ⅛ cup grated parmesan cheese
- ½ teaspoon dried thyme
- ¼ cup melted butter
- ½ cup Italian seasoned breadcrumbs
- ½ teaspoon dried basil
- ½ teaspoon salt

Directions:

- First, heat the oven to 400° F. Grease a baking sheet with cooking oil spray.
- Combine breadcrumbs, thyme, basil, salt, and Parmesan in a bowl.
- Place the melted butter in a bowl.
- Work with one piece of chicken at a time and dip the chicken in butter.
- Shake off excess butter, dredge in the breadcrumbs, and place on the prepared baking sheet. Do not overlap the chicken pieces.

- Keep the baking sheet in the oven and set the timer for about 20 minutes or until brown on the outside and cooked inside.

- Serve it hot with any dip you like.

(61) Baked Chicken Wings

Serves: 4

Ingredients:
- 1 ½ pounds of chicken wings
- 1 tablespoon of cooking oil of your choice
- 1 tablespoon BBQ sauce or more to taste
- 2 cloves garlic, peeled, minced

- Salt to taste
- Pepper to taste
- ¼ cup soy sauce
- ¼ cup honey
- Thinly sliced green onion to garnish (optional)

Directions:

- Preheat the oven to 350° F. Line a baking sheet with aluminum foil and grease the foil with some cooking oil spray.

- Sprinkle salt and pepper over the wings. Combine oil, BBQ sauce, garlic, soy sauce, and honey in a bowl. Add chicken wings and stir until well-coated.

- Place the chicken wings on the baking sheet without overlapping. Place the baking sheet in the oven and set the timer for about 50 minutes or until the chicken is cooked through and glaze is formed on the wings.

- Transfer the chicken onto a serving platter. Garnish with green onions and serve.

(62) Cheesy Ground Beef Pasta Skillet

Serves: 2

Ingredients:
- 1 cup ziti pasta
- ½ pound ground beef
- 2 cloves garlic, peeled, finely chopped
- ½ tablespoon Worcestershire sauce or more to taste
- ½ onion, chopped
- Salt to taste
- ½ tablespoon extra-virgin olive oil
- ¼ teaspoon pepper

- ½ teaspoon crushed red chili flakes (optional)
- 1 tablespoon tomato paste
- ¼ cup chopped parsley plus extra to garnish

Directions:

- Follow the directions given on the package of pasta and cook the pasta. Retain about ¼ - ½ cup of the cooked pasta water and drain the water from the pot. Do not rinse the pasta. Keep it aside for now.

- Place a skillet over high heat. Pour oil into the skillet and let it heat.

- When the oil is hot, add beef and stir often. As you stir, break the meat into crumbles. Cook until the meat is brown.

- Turn down the heat to medium heat. Add pepper and salt and stir.

- Add onion, garlic, Worcestershire sauce, parsley, chili flakes, tomato paste, and some retained water. Give the mixture a good stir. Check the consistency and add more retained water if you prefer.

- Cook for about 7 – 8 minutes or until the beef is cooked.

- Stir in the pasta and half the cheese. Heat thoroughly.

- Transfer into a serving dish. Sprinkle cheese and parsley on top. Cover the dish and let it sit for 5 minutes before serving.

(63) Cheesy Pepperoni Pizza Sticks

Serves: 10 (2 sticks per serving)

Ingredients:
- 2 refrigerated Pillsbury pizza crusts
- 20 mozzarella cheese sticks
- 1 teaspoon garlic powder
- Marinara sauce or any other sauce of your choice to serve (optional)
- 80 pepperoni slices
- 4 tablespoons butter
- 1 teaspoon dried parsley

Directions:

- Preheat the oven to 450° F. Grease 2 baking sheets by brushing lightly with oil.

- Unroll the pizza dough, one on each baking sheet. Cut each into 10 equal rectangular pieces.

- Place 4 pepperoni slices on each dough piece. Place a mozzarella cheese stick on each dough piece.

- Now roll the dough so that the cheese stick is enclosed. Press the sides to seal well.

- Melt butter in a microwave-safe bowl for about 30 seconds or until completely melted.

- Stir in parsley and garlic powder. Brush this mixture over the rolls.

- Place the baking sheet in the oven and set the timer for 10 – 12 minutes or until golden brown.

- Serve warm with marinara sauce.

(64) Pizza

Serves: 2 – 3

Ingredients:
- 8 ounces of pizza dough
- 3 ounces mozzarella cheese or Colby or Jack cheese, grated
- 1 – 2 tablespoons extra-virgin olive oil
- ¾ cup pizza sauce or marinara sauce
- Salt to taste
- Pepper to taste

For toppings: Choose your favorite

- Bell pepper slices
- Onion slices
- Tomato slices
- Cooked corn
- Mushroom slices
- Steamed vegetables of your choice like broccoli etc.
- Cooked, cubed, or shredded chicken
- Pepperoni slices
- Cured meat of your choice
- Cooked, crumbled sausage
- Pizza seasoning
- Any other toppings of your choice

Directions:

- Preheat the oven to 500° F. Prepare a rimmed baking sheet by lining it with parchment paper.

- Divide the dough into 2 equal portions and shape it into a ball. Roll the dough balls with a rolling pin into a circle of about 6 to 8 inches, depending on how thick the pizza is.

- Place them on the baking sheet leaving a gap between the 2 crusts.

- Spread pizza sauce over the dough. Sprinkle cheese on top of the sauce. Place the desired toppings and put the baking sheet into the oven.

- Bake for about 15 minutes or until the crust is cooked per your preference.

- Once the pizzas are cooked, take out the baking sheet and trickle olive oil over the pizzas. Season with pizza seasoning, salt, and pepper. Let them cool for about 5 minutes.

- Cut into wedges and serve.

(65) Pizza Casserole

Serves: 4 - 5

Ingredients:

- 8 ounces penne pasta
- 14 ounces of pizza sauce
- 1-ounce parmesan cheese
- 2 ounces green bell pepper, diced
- 2 ounces mushrooms, chopped
- ½ ounce black olives, sliced
- 2 cups shredded mozzarella cheese, divided

- 4 ounces tomatoes, diced
- ½ cup pepperonis
- 1 small onion, diced
- ½ pound ground Italian sausage

Directions:

- Preheat the oven to 375° F. Prepare a baking dish by greasing it with cooking oil spray.

- Follow the directions given on the package of pasta and cook the pasta.

- Meanwhile, place a skillet over medium heat. Add sausage and cook until the meat is cooked completely. Stir often. As you stir, break the meat into smaller pieces.

- Discard any cooked fat that is remaining in the pan. Turn off the heat.

- Combine the cooked pasta, pizza sauce, bell pepper, mushrooms, and one cup of mozzarella cheese, tomatoes, onions, and sausage in a bowl.

- Spread the mixture into the prepared baking dish. Sprinkle the remaining mozzarella cheese over the mixture.

- Top with pepperoni and olives. Finally, sprinkle Parmesan cheese on top and cover the dish with aluminum foil.

- Place the baking dish in the oven and set the timer for 30 minutes. Uncover and bake for another 5 – 8 minutes or until the cheese melts and is browned at a few spots.

(66) Beef Burgers

Serves: 8

Ingredients:
- 2 large eggs

- 1 teaspoon pepper
- 1 cup fine dry breadcrumbs
- ¼ teaspoon salt
- 2 pounds of ground beef
- Burger buns to serve
- Toppings of your choice

Directions:

- Add eggs, pepper, and salt into a bowl and whisk well. Next, stir in the beef and breadcrumbs using a fork or your hand.

- Thereafter, divide the mixture into 8 equal portions and form into patties of about ¾ inch thickness. You can cook the burgers in a pan or an oven.

- To cook in a pan: Place a nonstick pan over medium heat. When the pan is hot, place 4 patties and cook for 6 – 8 minutes.

- Flip the patties over and cook the other side for 6 – 8 minutes or until the internal temperature of the meat in the center of the patty shows 160° F on the meat thermometer.

- Remove the burgers onto a plate. Cook the remaining burgers similarly.

- Serve the burgers over buns with toppings of your choice.

(67) Tuna Sweet Corn Burgers

Serves: 8

Ingredients:

- 6 ounces of bread slices, torn
- 4 cans tuna in water, drained
- 6 green onions, finely chopped
- 4 tablespoons vegetable oil

- 2 cans (14 ounces each) of sweet corn, drained
- 1.8 ounces cheddar cheese, grated
- 2 eggs, beaten
- Burger bun or dinner rolls to serve
- Toppings of your choice

Directions:

- Place the bread pieces in the food processor bowl and process until crumbs are formed.

- Transfer the breadcrumbs to a bowl. Place half the corn in the food processor bowl and process until you get fine pieces. Transfer to the bowl of breadcrumbs.

- Add remaining corn, green onion, tuna, and cheese into the bowl of breadcrumbs and stir until well combined.

- Crack an egg into the mixture and mix well. Take out some mixture and try to shape it into a patty. If you can make a patty, you will not need to add the other egg. If you cannot shape the mixture into a patty, add the other egg and mix well.

- Divide the mixture into 8 equal portions and form into about ¾ inch thick patties.

- Place a nonstick pan over medium heat, and cook the patties over high heat for 5 minutes. Flip the patties over and cook the other side for 5 minutes.

- Serve over buns with toppings of your choice.

5. SWEET TREATS FOR BUSY TEENS

Dessert on the Go

(68) Tiramisu

Serves: 6

Ingredients:

- ¼ cup strong brewed coffee
- 8 ounces of cream cheese, softened
- 1 cup sour cream
- ¼ teaspoon vanilla extract
- ½ tablespoon unsweetened cocoa powder
- 1 tablespoon coffee liqueur
- 1/3 cup sugar
- ⅛ cup 2% milk
- 1 package (3 ounces) of ladyfingers, split

Directions:

- Mix coffee and liqueur in a bowl.
- Place cream cheese and sugar in another bowl. Beat with an electric hand mixer until well combined.
- Add sour cream, vanilla, and milk and beat until well combined.
- To assemble: Place half the ladyfingers on the bottom of a square pan. Do not grease the pan.

- Using a pastry brush, brush half the coffee mixture over the ladyfingers.
- Spread half the cream cheese mixture over the ladyfingers.
- Repeat the layers once again.
- Cover the pan with cling wrap and place the pan in the refrigerator.
- Chill for at least 8 hours. Divide into six equal portions and place on small plates.
- Garnish with cocoa and serve.

(69) Hot Fudge Pudding Cake

Serves: 4

Ingredients:

- 10 tablespoons granulated sugar divided
- ¼ cup unsweetened cocoa powder, divided
- ⅛ teaspoon salt
- 3 tablespoons unsalted butter
- ¼ cup packed brown sugar
- ½ cup all-purpose flour
- 1 teaspoon baking powder
- ¼ cup milk
- ¾ teaspoon vanilla extract
- ½ cup plus ⅛ cup hot water

To serve:
- Vanilla ice cream (optional)

Directions:

- Place butter in a microwave-safe bowl and melt for about 20 seconds.

- The water should be hot and not boiling.

- Preheat the oven to 350° F.

- Place 6 tablespoons of granulated sugar, 2 tablespoons of cocoa, salt, flour, and baking powder in a mixing bowl. Stir until well combined.

- Add butter, milk, and vanilla and beat with an electric hand mixer until smooth.

- Grease a small baking dish (about 6 inches) with cooking oil spray.

- Spoon the batter into the dish.

- Combine brown sugar, remaining granulated sugar, and cocoa in a bowl. Sprinkle this on top of the batter.

- Drizzle the hot water all over the batter. Make sure you do not stir the batter.

- Place the baking dish in the oven and set the timer for 30 – 40 minutes or until moist in the middle and set around the edges.

- Take out the baking dish and let it cool for about 15 minutes before serving.

- Serve the pudding in bowls. Make sure to serve the most part from the center along with the set part. You can serve the pudding with vanilla ice cream.

(70) Oreo Poke Cake

Serves: 8 – 9

Ingredients:

- ½ box (from a 15.25 ounces box) of chocolate cake mix
- All the ingredients that are mentioned on the box of the chocolate mix (use only half of each of the ingredients)
- 1 cup cold milk
- 5 Oreo cookies, crushed
- ½ box (from a 3.4 ounces box) of vanilla or white chocolate instant pudding mix
- ½ carton (from a 12 ounces carton) of frozen whipped topping, thawed

Directions:

- Follow the instructions on the cake mix box and prepare the cake. Suppose there are 2 eggs given on the box. Use only one as you are using only ½ the box. So use half the quantity of all the ingredients mentioned in the box.

- Once the cake is made, let it cool for about 15 minutes. Then, take a wooden skewer and prick holes in the cake.

- Combine pudding mix and milk and make the pudding following the directions given on the package.

- Spoon the pudding on top of the cake and spread it evenly with a spatula, pressing the pudding into the holes as you apply.

- Chill for at least 2 hours.

- Spoon the whipped topping on the cake and chill until further use.

- Scatter Oreo cookie crumbs on top. Cut into slices and serve.

(71) Chick Fil- A Frosted Coffee

Serves: 2

Ingredients:

- 1 cup of brewed coffee, chilled
- 4 cups vanilla ice cream

Directions:

- Blend ice cream and coffee in a blender until frothy.
- Pour into 2 tall glasses and serve right away.

(72) Vanilla Ice Cream

Serves: 10 - 12

Ingredients:

- 2 cans (14 ounces each) of sweetened condensed milk
- 4 cups heavy cream, chilled
- 4 teaspoons vanilla extract

Directions:

- Take 2 loaf pans or freezer-safe containers and place parchment paper on the bottom of the pan.

- Take 2 loaf pans or freezer-safe containers and place parchment paper on the bottom of the pan.
- Chill 2 bowls in the freezer for about 15 minutes.
- Add vanilla and condensed milk to one of the bowls and stir until well combined.
- Pour the heavy cream into the other chilled bowl and whip with an electric hand mixer until stiff peaks are formed. Be careful not to overbeat, or you will end up with butter.
- Add whipped cream into the bowl with condensed milk and fold gently.
- If you want to add other flavorings like berries, chocolate chips, etc., you can add them now.
- Spoon the mixture into the pans. Keep them covered with cling wrap. Freeze for 4 hours if you want soft serve consistency and longer if you want to firm ice cream.

(73) Easy Apple Cobbler

Serves: 12

Ingredients:

- 2 cans Pillsbury cinnamon rolls, cut each roll into 4 equal pieces
- 1 teaspoon ground cinnamon (optional)
- 42 ounces of apple pie filling

Directions:

- Preheat the oven to 375° F. Take a large baking dish and spray some cooking oil into the dish.

- Combine cinnamon roll pieces, cinnamon, and apple pie filling in a large bowl.

- Transfer the mixture to the baking dish. Place the baking dish in the oven and bake for about 20 to 25 minutes or until golden brown.

- Cool for around 15 minutes. You will find frosting in the can of a cinnamon roll. Spoon the frosting on top and spread it evenly.

- Serve.

(74) Chocolate Almond Clusters

Serves: 7 - 8

Ingredients:

- 6 ounces almond bark, roughly chopped
- ½ - 1 teaspoon coarse sea salt
- 1 cup whole raw almonds

Directions:

- Start with preparing a baking sheet by lining it with parchment paper.
- Then, melt the almond bark in a microwave-safe bowl for about 60 – 90 seconds or until completely melted. Stir every 30 seconds.
- Stir in the almonds. Place a tablespoonful of the mixture on the baking sheet in a heap. Do this until all the mixture is placed.
- Scatter coarse salt on top of each heap. In a while, they will harden. To speed up the process, chill for 10 to 15 minutes.
- Transfer into an airtight container and place in the refrigerator or at room temperature.

(75) Dole Whip

Serves: 2

Ingredients:

- 4 cups frozen, canned, small pineapple chunks
- 8 ounces of pineapple juice
- 2 scoops vanilla ice cream

Directions:

- Add pineapple, pineapple juice, and ice cream into the food processor bowl and process until smooth and soft serve consistency.

- Divide into bowls and serve right away. You can make an extra whip, pour it into ice cube trays, and freeze it until used.

- Remove the frozen cubes and add to the food processor bowl. Process until smooth and soft serve consistency.

- Serve.

(76) Peanut Butter Rice Krispie Treats

Serves: 6 – 8

Ingredients:

- 2 tablespoons unsalted butter
- 4 tablespoons peanut butter
- 4 ounces of chocolate chips
- 5 ounces of mini marshmallows
- 3 cups Rice Krispie cereal
- 1 teaspoon vegetable oil

Directions:

- Spray a small, square baking pan with some cooking oil spray.

- Combine butter, peanut butter, and mini marshmallows in a saucepan and place it over low heat. Stir often until the mixture melts. Turn off the heat.

- Add rice Krispies and stir until well combined.

- Transfer the mixture to the baking pan and press with greased hands until it is even.

- Melt the chocolate chips in a microwave-safe bowl for about 2 minutes or until it melts. Stir every 30 seconds.

- Whisk in the oil. Drizzle the melted chocolate all over the Rice Krispies mixture.

- Let it cool for about 2 hours. Chop into squares and place in an airtight container at room temperature. Use within 3 days.

(77) Chocolate Pudding

Serves: 6

Ingredients:

- 4 cups of milk of your choice
- ½ cup Dutch cocoa powder
- 1 cup milk of your choice mixed with 6 tablespoons cornstarch
- 1 ½ tablespoons vanilla extract
- 1/3 teaspoon salt
- ⅔ cup sweetener of your choice like sugar, honey, maple syrup, etc.
- 6 ounces chocolate chips or broken chocolate bar

Directions:

- Add milk, cocoa, salt, and sweetener into a saucepan and place it over medium heat. Stir on and off until the mixture is slightly hot.

- Stir the cornstarch mixture and pour it into the saucepan. Keep stirring until it starts boiling rapidly. Let it simmer rapidly for 2 minutes. Keep on stirring.

- Turn down the heat to low heat and cook for 1 minute.

- Add chocolate and vanilla and stir until the chocolate melts completely.

- Pour the mixture into a container. Cover and chill for 6 – 8 hours at least before serving.

Conclusion

Thank you once again for choosing this book. I hope you enjoyed the delicious and easy recipes given in this book. By now, you would have realized that cooking is easy. Also, it is quite a fun activity. Once you know what to do, cooking becomes extremely simple.

Learning to cook will make you feel self-sufficient, increase your quotient of personal satisfaction, act as an outlet for stress, improve your self-confidence, and make you feel independent. It also helps improve your relationship with food, produces better and healthier food choices, and gives you control over what and how much you eat.

Combining these factors makes cooking one of the basic life skills anyone can acquire. Also, there is no such thing as the right time or age to learn to cook. Instead, it is about having the right mindset. Once you start cooking for yourself, you will realize how simple it is.

While cooking, paying attention to the basic cooking techniques and learning them is needed. This, coupled with a little meal prep, further makes the process easy.

Spend a couple of hours over the weakened planning of the meals for the upcoming week. Gather the needed ingredients and stock the pantry. You can also batch-cook recipes you and your family love. Then, freeze the meals, and delicious home-cooked meals will be ready within no time during the week. From comfort food to indulgent desserts, you can cook whatever you want. However, the first step is always to learn the basics. Once you get the basics right, cooking itself becomes simple.

All the recipes in this book are divided into different categories for convenience. This book has everything you need to start, from breakfast and quick meals to snacks, soups, salads, and desserts. Whether you want breakfast before heading to school or a full-fledged meal for your family, this book will guide you. You were also introduced to what meal prep is and the basic cooking techniques everyone must know. Once you are armed with this information, you can cook like a pro quickly!

This book introduced you to various beginner-friendly recipes perfect for teens. All the recipes are easy and can be cooked in no time. By now, you would have realized that you don't have to spend hours together in the kitchen to cook.

Instead, you need the right ingredients, a tried and tested recipe, and an interest in cooking. Once all this is in place, cooking is easy and incredibly fun. You will discover a variety of recipes that will help you whip up delicious meals like a pro! So, if you want to blow your loved ones away with delicious home-cooked meals or become self-sufficient, start using the recipes given in this book.

Before you start cooking, spend a little time carefully reading through the ingredients needed and the steps to follow. Be sure to complete this step if you want to cook delicious meals. Once you know what's to be done, cooking automatically becomes easy. This also ensures you don't miss out on any steps. Also, there are no hard and fast rules about cooking.

However, it is recommended to stock the instructions in the recipes. Once you get the hang of cooking, are comfortable with the basic cooking techniques, and understand different flavor combinations, it is time to let your imagination run wild. Don't hesitate to experiment a little in the kitchen. This is not only fun but exciting too.

So, are you eager to start cooking? If yes, what are you waiting for?

There is no time like the present to do this!

Thank you, and all the best!

Dr. Fanatomy

TeeNavigator Series

Notes

Notes

www.ingramcontent.com/pod-product-compliance
Lightning Source LLC
Chambersburg PA
CBHW050317010526
44107CB00055B/2281